cooking the Swiss way

From the Alpine region of Ticino, noodles with saffron and garden-style vegetable salad bring Italian flavor to traditional Swiss cooking. (Recipes are on pages 33 and 34.)

cooking the Swiss way

HELGA HUGHES

PHOTOGRAPHS BY ROBERT L. AND DIANE WOLFE

easy menu
ethnic
cookbooks

Lerner Publications Company ▪ Minneapolis

Editor: Barbara L. King

Additional photographs and illustrations courtesy of Laura
Westlund, pp. 6, 15, 27, 39, borders; Swiss National Tourist
Office, pp. 9, 10, 13, 14, 17.

**To my sister Lore, chef at the Bavarian Schloss
Griefenstein, for her valuable baking tips; to my
childhood friends Anni and Margarete for gifts of
food used in testing some recipes in this book; and to
my cousin Erika and my brother's wife, Inge, for their
valuable help.**

Library of Congress Cataloguing-in-Publication Data

Hughes, Helga.
    Cooking the Swiss way / by Helga Hughes ;
  photographs by Robert L. & Diane Wolfe.
      p.   cm. — (Easy menu ethnic cookbooks)
    Includes index.
    ISBN 0-8225-0930-X
    1. Cookery, Swiss—Juvenile literature. 2. Switzerland—Social life
and customs—Juvenile literature. [1. Cookery, Swiss. 2. Switzerland—
Social life and customs.] I. Wolfe, Robert L., ill. II. Wolfe, Diane, ill.
III. Title. IV. Series.
TX723.5.S9H84   1995
641.59494—dc20   94-25397
                                     CIP
                                     AC

Manufactured in the United States of America

1 2 3 4 5 6 I/JR 00 99 98 97 96 95

Peek-in-the-Oven Casserole is a hearty combination of potatoes, sausage, eggs, and cheese in one delicious main dish. (Recipe is on page 35.)

CONTENTS

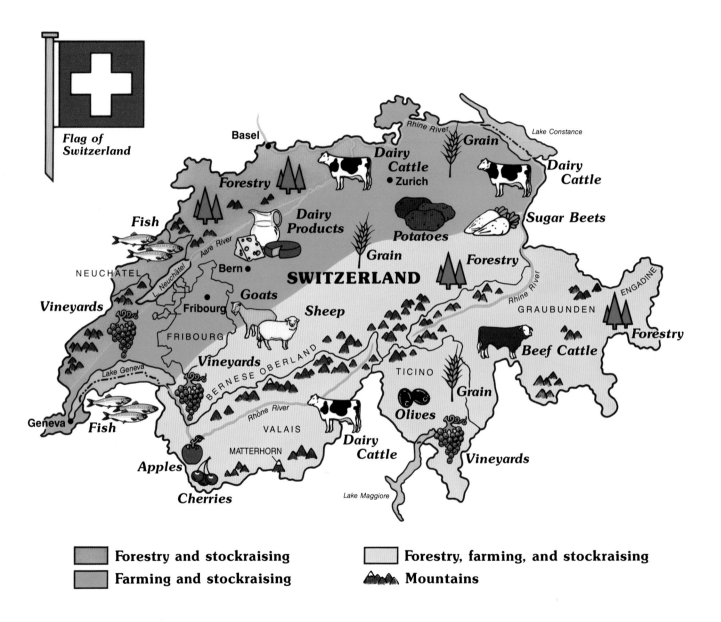

Flag of
Switzerland

Basel

Rhine River
Lake Constance

Forestry
Dairy
Cattle
• Zurich
Grain
Dairy
Cattle

Fish

Dairy
Products
Potatoes
Sugar Beets

NEUCHÂTEL
Bern •
Grain
SWITZERLAND
Forestry
ENGADINE

Vineyards
Goats
Fribourg •
Sheep
Rhine River
GRAUBUNDEN
Forestry

FRIBOURG
Vineyards
BERNESE OBERLAND
Beef Cattle

Lake Geneva
TICINO

Fish
Rhône River
Olives
Grain

Geneva •
Fish
VALAIS
Dairy
Cattle
Vineyards

Apples
MATTERHORN

Cherries
Lake Maggiore

Forestry and stockraising   Forestry, farming, and stockraising
Farming and stockraising   Mountains

INTRODUCTION

The movie *Heidi* accurately pictured Switzerland as a land of magical variety: snow-capped mountains, green valleys, historic castles, charming villages, shimmering lakes, and bubbling streams. I experienced this fairy-tale land for the first time when I was growing up in Germany. On a school trip to Switzerland, we hiked up to an Alpine farm to watch *Sennern* (herders) make cheese. Along the way, we saw farmers working in the fields. They wore traditional Swiss clothing, the men in plain cotton shirts and black knee-length britches with suspenders and the women in embroidered cotton blouses and colorful ruffled skirts. At times we would hear the distant echo of yodeling from higher up the mountain and had fun trying to imitate the sound.

Toward the end of the day, we watched the setting sun color the snow-capped Alpine peaks with splashes of crimson. In the distance, we could hear the deep, melodious sounds of alphorns, the long wooden horns used to summon the cows from the mountainsides. Mingled with the horns' strange sounds was the ringing of cowbells as the herds made their way down the slopes to find shelter for the night.

The next day, we visited a factory to watch the production of one of Switzerland's biggest exports—chocolate. As we walked to the factory, we could smell the delicious aroma of sweetened cocoa and milk—milk from the cows we had seen in the valleys. In the factory, I gazed in awe at the rows of display cases that contained over 300 varieties of chocolate candy. To our delight, we were each given a memento of foil-wrapped chocolate cowbells. The wrapping was stamped with a greeting in the country's four languages: Swiss German, French, Italian, and Romansh, an ancient language similar to Latin.

The Land

Switzerland was originally settled by tribes from the north. Until the country was conquered by Rome in 58 B.C., the largest group of settlers were the Celtic *Helvetii,* in the northwestern part of the country. Some people still refer to Switzerland as Helvetia.

After the decline of the Roman empire, conquering forces came from Germany, France, and Austria. Each country left an imprint on Swiss cooking. Their influence led to unique recipes now known as Swiss, such as *fondue* (melted cheese dip), *Rösti* (fried potatoes), and *Leckerli* (cookies).

The country's official name is the Swiss Confederation, although this name is seldom used in conversation. About half the size of Indiana, Switzerland is one of Europe's smallest countries both in area and population. Even so, Switzerland is one of the world's major commercial and financial centers.

Landlocked Switzerland is surrounded by France, Germany, Liechtenstein, Austria, and Italy. The mountain range known as the Swiss Alps has many peaks over 13 thousand feet high and covers almost half of the land area. The most famous peak, the Matterhorn, reaches 14,692 feet into the sky.

The Alps receive a heavy annual snowfall that provides an abundance of pure water for homes, fields, and Switzerland's 1,500 lakes. The largest of these, Lake Geneva, is big enough to be called an inland sea.

Although the Swiss fought in foreign wars in early times, the country has been neutral since the early 15th century. By never taking sides during international conflicts, Switzerland enjoys peace when other countries are at war. In the 19th century, however, Swiss compassion for those wounded in war led to the formation of the International Red Cross. As a tribute to Switzerland, the colors of the famous Red Cross symbol are the reverse of the Swiss flag.

Switzerland is divided into 26 *cantons* (states). Each canton has its own style of architecture. The Bernese Oberland region has chalets with low-pitched roofs and wide eaves. In the Valais canton, barns are elevated above the ground on blocks to keep mice out of grain stores. In the Engadine region of the

The Swiss Alps, possibly Switzerland's most famous feature, cover more than half of the country and attract tourists from around the world.

eastern Graubünden canton, houses are covered with stucco and beautifully decorated with floral, pastoral, or geometric designs. Some even have paintings of the everyday activities of dairy farming.

The People

Most people in Swiss cities live in comfortable, modern apartments. Their balconies overflow with colorful flowers in the spring, summer, and fall. In the 19th century, a Swiss doctor named Daniel Schreber convinced city authorities to set aside land for gardening. Even in the big cities of Zurich, Basel, and Geneva, families grow their own fresh vegetables and fruits in small plots called *Schrebergarten*.

Dr. A. Vogel, the "Swiss Nature Doctor," wrote many books on gathering fresh elderberries, rosehips, dandelion, chamomile, and flowers from linden trees to make health foods such as preserves, honey, and herbal teas. Entire families are often seen in Switzerland with knapsacks on their backs, combing the woods to collect the natural bounty.

Humorous costumes and festive food are part of the annual Basel carnival.

The Food

Food plays an important part in the lives of the Swiss people as a centerpiece for family togetherness. A proverb often displayed in kitchens and dining rooms, *Essen und Trinken halt Leib and Seele zusammen,* means "Food and drink keep body and soul together."

Swiss people cook in two distinctly different ways: haute (high) cuisine and true (traditional) cuisine. Haute cuisine, a gourmet style of cooking originally from France, is found in wealthy homes, top international hotels, and expensive restaurants. Haute cuisine is refined and extravagant. This cooking style employs precise carving and dicing techniques, elaborate garnishes, rich sauces, and lots of butter and cream. Haute cuisine's complex dishes use expensive ingredients such as truffles (a rare underground mushroom) and *foie gras* (goose liver).

The haute cuisine dish *Veal Cordon Bleu* is veal stuffed with ham and cheese, then seasoned, breaded, and fried. In true Swiss cuisine, on the other hand, this same veal becomes *Plätzli,* a simple Swiss dish of veal that is seasoned, breaded, and fried.

True Swiss cuisine embraces regional, seasonal, and festive food specialties. This cooking style developed long ago through the skill and imagination of Swiss cooks. Before the Swiss Alps became a tourist attraction, the country was poor and cooks had little to work with. The old recipes used garden vegetables, such as beans, cabbages, carrots, potatoes, and turnips. They included barley, corn, millet, and spelt—a type of wheat that was one of the first grains known to humans. Apples, berries, pears, and other fruit were also popular ingredients, used fresh during the summer and preserved or dried for the winter. Swiss cooks planned whole menus around these fruits in stews, casseroles, and breads. To their vegetables, they added dairy products in the form of butter, milk, and cheese.

The recipes in this book are some examples of true Swiss cuisine. Try these 16 traditional dishes yourself and discover the flavorful variety of foods enjoyed in Swiss homes every day.

BEFORE YOU BEGIN

Cooking any dish, plain or fancy, is easier and more fun if you are familiar with the utensils, terms, and ingredients used in a recipe. Swiss cooking makes use of some ingredients that you may not know. You should be familiar with the special terms used in this book before you start cooking. Study the following "dictionary" of special ingredients and terms very carefully. Then read through each recipe from beginning to end before trying it.

Now you are ready to shop for ingredients and to organize the cookware you will need. (Expensive spices can often be purchased loose, so you can buy only as much as you'll need.) Once you have assembled everything, you can begin to cook. It is also important to read *The Careful Cook* on page 44 before you start. Following these rules will make your cooking experience safe, fun, and easy.

COOKING UTENSILS

double boiler – Two saucepans that fit together so that the contents in the upper pan can be heated by boiling water in the lower pan

fondue fork – A long-stemmed fork

fondue pot – A small pot with rounded sides and a handle that is used to melt cheese or chocolate as a sauce, or to heat oil to cook small pieces of food. Traditional fondue pots are made of cast iron or enamel and sit on a small stand over a single flame. Electric fondue pots are recommended for safety and ease of use.

grater – A utensil with sharp-edged holes, used to cut food into tiny pieces

ladle – A deep-bowled spoon that is used for transferring soups and sauces

pastry brush – A small brush used to spread liquids such as melted butter, egg whites, and glazes on breads, cookies, etc.

rolling pin – A heavy, cylindrical tool used for rolling out dough

sieve – A basket of fine mesh used for straining liquids and sifting powdered solids

slotted spoon – A spoon with small openings in the bowl. It is used to remove solid food from liquid.

steaming basket – A metal basket that fits inside a saucepan and allows food to be cooked with steam

COOKING TERMS

beat – To stir rapidly in a circular motion

boil – To heat a liquid over high heat until bubbles form and rise rapidly to the surface

brown – To cook food quickly with high heat so that the food's surface turns an even brown

dash – A very small amount of seasoning dispensed by a quick shake of a container

fillet – A piece of meat or fish with the bones removed

garnish – To decorate with a small piece of food such as parsley

grate – To cut into tiny pieces by rubbing the food against a grater

knead – To work dough by pressing it with the palms, pushing it outward, and folding it over on itself

marinate – To soak a food in seasoned liquid to tenderize and flavor it

Many restaurants in Switzerland serve traditional Swiss dishes.

A group of hikers stop for a picnic by one of Switzer-land's many waterfalls.

pinch – A small amount of seasoning, usually what you can pick up between your thumb and forefinger

poach – To simmer food in liquid

preheat – To allow an oven to warm up to the required temperature before putting food into it

sauté – To fry in a small amount of oil or fat, stirring or turning the food to prevent burning

sift – To put an ingredient, such as flour or sugar, through a sifter to break up any lumps

simmer – To cook over low heat in liquid kept just below the boiling point. (Bubbles may occasionally rise to the surface.)

steam – To cook food with the steam from boiling water

whip – To beat an ingredient, such as cream or egg white, until light and fluffy

SPECIAL INGREDIENTS

almond extract – A liquid made from the oil of almonds, used to give an almond flavor to food

basil – A rich, fragrant herb used fresh or dried to flavor foods such as salads and Italian dishes

bouillon cube – A compressed mixture of spices, seasoning, and oils used to make broth

caraway seeds – A strongly flavored seed from a plant in the carrot family that is often used in breads and cheeses

chives – Green stalks of a plant in the onion family that is used as a garnish and a flavoring

cider vinegar – A golden vinegar made from apple cider

cinnamon – A spice made from the bark of a tree in the laurel family. It is available both ground and in sticks.

cloves – Dried buds from a small evergreen tree that can be used whole or ground to flavor food

dill weed – A pungent herb, the dried leaves of which are used to flavor food

Emmentaler cheese – An ivory-colored hard cheese with cherry-sized holes that is aged about six months. In Switzerland, the cheese is made from milk of cows that graze the upper Emmental meadows. The name may be spelled "Emmenthaler" or "Emmental."

fettucine – Pasta cut into narrow strips about ¼ inch wide

garlic – An herb whose distinctive flavor is used in many dishes. Each bulb can be broken into several small sections called cloves. Remove the brittle, papery covering around each clove before chopping it up.

ground ginger – The ground, dried underground stem of a reed-like plant with a peppery, piquant flavor

Gruyère cheese – A hard, tangy Swiss cheese that is aged about 12 months and made from milk of cows grazed in the Gruyère area.

imitation rum extract – A condensed liquid of corn syrup and other oils used to flavor sweets

kale – A vegetable, related to the cabbage, with loose, curly, dark green or purple leaves

leek – An herb in the onion family, but smaller and milder in taste than an onion. The bulbs and greens of leeks are used to flavor soups, stews, and sauces.

marjoram – A fragrant herb of the mint family used either fresh or dried

nutmeg – A fragrant spice, used either whole or ground, often in desserts

paprika – A dried herb made from sweet red pepper, used for flavoring and coloring food

Parmesan cheese – A hard, golden yellow Italian cheese usually grated for topping savory dishes

parsley – A green leafy herb used as a seasoning and as a garnish

pickling spice – A mixture of mustard seeds, bay leaves, black peppercorns, and other spices used for pickling and marinating

pimento – A sweet, red pepper that is available in cans or jars and is often used to add color to food

rolled oats – Oats that have been steamed and rolled until flat, after having the outer skin or husk removed

saffron – Dried, orange stigmas (parts of a flower that receive pollen) from a species of crocus. Saffron is used to flavor food and to color it a pale yellow.

sage – A strongly flavored herb used in soups, poultry stuffing, and stews

spelt flakes – Commercially prepared flakes made from a variety of wheat kernel. Spelt flakes can be purchased at natural food stores.

thyme – A fragrant herb used either fresh or dried

turbinado sugar – Unrefined, golden-colored sugar, often referred to as "raw sugar"

turmeric – A yellow, aromatic spice from the root of the turmeric plant

vanilla sugar – A mixture of white sugar and ground vanilla beans that is used in desserts

white pepper – Ground peppercorns that have had their hulls removed. White pepper is milder in flavor than black pepper.

whole wheat flour – Flour that is ground from whole grain kernels, giving it a darker color than highly refined white flour

Every spring the Swiss celebrate *Alpaufzug,* **or "moving to the Alps." During this festival, herders bring dairy cattle back to high mountain pastures. Special dishes made of dairy products highlight the festivities.**

A SWISS MENU

The Swiss eat a hearty breakfast even though their main dinner meal is at midday. *Z'vieri,* the four o'clock break, is the time for coffee, desserts, and pastries, while the evening meal is a light supper. The recipes in this menu are identified as Swiss German (G), French (F), Italian (I), or Romansh (R) to represent the language spoken in the original recipe's canton. A selection for a typical day of Swiss meals would be made from the menu that follows.

ENGLISH	SWISS	PRONUNCIATION
Breakfast	*Frühstück (G)*	*FREW-shtook*
Fried Apples and Bread Slices	Öpfel Bröisi (G)	UHP-ful BROI-si
Cereal Bircher-Benner Style	Birchermüsli (G)	Bir-sher MEWZ-lee
Alpine Omelet	Cholermues (R)	KOH-ler-mus
Dinner	*Mittagessen (G)*	*MIT-tahg-ehs-en*
I		
Cabbage Soup	Kabissuppe (G)	KAH-bis-ZOOP-eh
Baked Chicken and Vegetables	Mistkratzerli und Gemüse (G)	MEEST-crah-tzer-lee unt Ge-MEW-zeh
Fried Potatoes	Rösti (G)	RUHS-tee
Onion Salad	Zibelsalat (G)	SEE-behl-zah-LAHT

ENGLISH	SWISS	PRONUNCIATION
II		
Tomatoes Fribourg Style	Tomates Fribourgeoises (F)	Toh-MAHT free-boor-ZHWAZ
Poached Perch Fillets	Filets de Perche (F)	Fee-LAY duh PAIRSH
III		
Garden-Style Vegetable Salad	Insalata Giardiniera (I)	IN-sah-LAH-tah Jyar-dee-NYAIR-ah
Noodles with Saffron	Pasta allo Zafferano (I)	PAHS-tah ah-loh DZAH-feh-RAH-noh
IV		
Peek-in-the-Oven Casserole	Ofenguck (G)	OH-fen-gook
Desserts	***Nachtisch (G)***	***NAKH-tish***
Cherry Bread Pudding	Chriesibrägel (R)	Kri-zee-BRAHG-uhl
Cookies from the City of Basel	Basler Leckerli (G)	BAHZ-ler LECK-er-lee
Chocolate Fondue	Schokolade Fondue (G)	SHO-KO-lah-deh fawn-DOO
Supper	***Abendessen (G)***	***AH-bend-ehs-en***
Valais-Style Fondue	Fondue Valais (F)	Fawn-DOO vah-LAY

Breakfast time in Switzerland offers a number of appetizing ways to start the day. Try cereal Bircher-Benner style (left, recipe on page 22) or fried apples and bread slices (right).

BREAKFAST
Frühstück (G)
Le Petit Déjeuner (F)
La Prima Colazione (I)

A proverb from the German-speaking regions, *Ein Mann ißt wie er arbeitet,* means "A man works as he eats." Hardworking farmers eat substantial breakfasts of porridge, hearty fried potato dishes, or rich, thick soups. Herders prefer bread and cheese, filled omelets, or milk, fresh whey, and dried fruits.

In Swiss cities, breakfast consists of fresh rolls spread with butter and preserves. Popular with children are crescent-shaped pastries called horns that are filled with jam, nuts and honey, or bittersweet chocolate. Favorite beverages are hot chocolate, herbal teas, or *café au lait* (hot milk and coffee).

Most country and city dwellers eat a second breakfast of open-faced meat or cheese sandwiches around 9:00 A.M. The Swiss call this meal *Z'nueni,* a name derived from the number nine.

Fried Apples and Bread Slices
Öpfel Bröisi

4 tablespoons unsalted butter or margarine
2 apples, peeled, cored, quartered and sliced thin
dash cinnamon
2 tablespoons turbinado sugar or brown sugar
4 slices white bread, toasted and cut into ¾-inch squares

1. Heat 2 tablespoons butter in a large skillet over medium-high heat. Add apple slices and sprinkle with cinnamon and sugar. Cook the apples for 5 minutes, turning frequently with a spatula.
2. Add bread squares and turn heat to medium low. Continue to cook for another 5 minutes, stirring frequently.
3. Place apple and bread slices on serving platter and top with remaining butter. Serve immediately.

Serves 4

Cereal Bircher-Benner Style
Birchermüsli

This cereal was first served in Dr. Bircher-Benner's Zurich clinic in the early 20th century. His patients enjoyed it so much that they took the recipe home.

1 cup old-fashioned rolled oats
1 cup toasted spelt flakes (or increase oats to 2 cups)
½ teaspoon cinnamon
1 teaspoon vanilla sugar
¼ cup maple syrup
¼ cup chopped nuts
⅓ cup raisins
1 apple
milk or yogurt to taste

1. Preheat oven to 300°.
2. In a medium-sized bowl, combine oat and spelt flakes. Sprinkle with cinnamon and vanilla sugar and pour maple syrup in a circle on top. Stir until mixed well.
3. Generously coat a large baking sheet with no-stick cooking spray. With the spoon, spread cereal evenly on the sheet. Bake until flakes are golden brown (about 15 minutes), stirring occasionally.
4. Remove cereal from oven and allow to cool. Pour cereal into an airtight container and add nuts and raisins, mixing well. The cereal may be stored in the refrigerator for up to a week.
5. To serve, divide cereal into 4 bowls. Peel and core an apple and grate it on top of cereal. Add milk or yogurt to taste.

Serves 4

Alpine Omelet
Cholermues

1 6-ounce package dried fruit bits
1½ cups water
1 tablespoon juice of fresh lemon
2½ tablespoons unsalted butter or margarine
2 teaspoons cornstarch
1 tablespoon maple syrup or honey
6 tablespoons white flour
4 eggs
1 cup half-and-half
dash nutmeg

1. In a small bowl, soak fruit bits with water and lemon juice for several hours or overnight. Drain fruit and reserve liquid.

2. In a small pan, melt 1 tablespoon butter over medium-high heat. Add cornstarch, stirring quickly. Stir in syrup or honey and the water from the fruit. Stir until mixture is thick and smooth. Add fruit and simmer on low heat while making the omelet.

3. In a large bowl, whip together flour, eggs, half-and-half, and nutmeg until frothy. Cover bowl with a towel and place in refrigerator for 15 minutes. Remove and whip mixture once more.

4. Turn heat to medium high under a large frying pan. Melt 1½ tablespoons butter and add egg mixture. Cover, turn heat to low, and cook for 7 to 8 minutes—until omelet is light brown on the bottom.

5. With a wooden spoon, break the omelet into bite-sized pieces and turn them over. Turn heat off and allow egg mixture to become firm on the bottom. Serve immediately with stewed fruits.

Serves 4

Creamy eggs are a perfect match for sweet fruit in an Alpine omelet from the Romansh districts.

DINNER
Mittagessen (G)
Le Déjeuner (F)
Il Pranzo (I)

Most Swiss families eat their largest meal of the day at noon. Schools, shops, and factories close around that time to let people enjoy their meal together. On farms, families gather in the fields to share a hot dinner. A typical menu might start with onion, cheese, or vegetable soup followed by vegetables and a main dish of poultry, veal, beef, or fish. The main dish is served with potatoes in German- and French-speaking cantons, but with pasta in Italian-speaking cantons.

Swiss cabbage soup is a warm, wholesome way to begin a meal.

Cabbage Soup
Kabissuppe

The cheese topping for this soup will vary from canton to canton—Gruyère in French cantons, Emmentaler in German cantons, and Parmesan in Italian ones.

 2 bacon slices, chopped
 2 tablespoons minced yellow onion
 4 cups thinly sliced white cabbage
 ½ teaspoon dried sage
 ¼ teaspoon pepper
 ¼ teaspoon salt
 1 tablespoon white flour
 6 cups water
 1 chicken bouillon cube
 ½ cup long-grain brown rice
 4 tablespoons grated Emmentaler
     cheese

1. Fry bacon in a large pot over medium heat. Add onions and cook until they are soft. Add cabbage, sage, pepper, and salt. Sauté until cabbage is lightly browned (about 5 minutes). Then add flour, stirring to coat cabbage.
2. Add water and bouillon cube, turn heat to high, and bring to a boil.
3. Add rice and turn heat to low. Simmer, covered, for 40 minutes.
4. Ladle soup into 4 large soup bowls and top each with a tablespoon of grated cheese before serving.

Serves 4

Baked Chicken and Vegetables
Mistkratzerli und Gemüse

**4 chicken breasts with wings attached
    (about 3¼ pounds)**
  salt and pepper to taste
1 teaspoon ground sage
2 tablespoons butter or margarine

Stuffing:
 2 cups water
½ teaspoon thyme
 2 tablespoons dried fruit bits
 2 tablespoons maple syrup
 1 chicken bouillon cube
 **8 slices dark bread (whole wheat, rye,
    or multigrain), toasted and torn
    into small pieces**
 1 egg
¼ teaspoon salt
  dash black pepper

1. Preheat oven to 400°.
2. Rinse chicken with cold water and drain well. Salt and pepper chicken on all sides. Sprinkle with sage.
3. Coat a large, deep baking dish with no-stick cooking spray and place chicken, wing side up, in the dish.
4. Cover dish with aluminum foil and bake for 45 minutes. Remove foil, dot chicken with butter, and bake for another 15 minutes.
5. To make a stock for the stuffing, pour water into a medium-sized saucepan and add ¼ teaspoon thyme, dried fruits, 1 tablespoon syrup, and bouillon cube. Bring to a boil, then reduce heat to medium low. Simmer, covered, for 15 minutes.
6. Place toast pieces in a medium-sized bowl and pour stock over them. Break the egg into the bowl and add remaining thyme, syrup, salt, and pepper. Mix well.
7. Remove baking dish from oven and transfer chicken to a board or plate. Drain off all but ¼ cup of pan juices.

8. Spoon 4 equal mounds of stuffing into the baking dish. Set chicken, wing sides up, on top of mounds. Cover with foil, return to oven, and bake for 30 minutes.
9. Remove from oven and transfer stuffing mounds, with chicken on top, to a serving platter.

Serves 4

Vegetables:
½ **pound green kale (about 20 leaves), washed**
3 **tablespoons butter or margarine**
¼ **teaspoon white pepper**
   dash nutmeg
1 **tablespoon white flour**
1 **cup water**
2 **medium carrots, cleaned and coarsely grated (about 1 cup)**

1. Cut away the center ribs of the kale along the stems. Roll each leaf and slice into ¼-inch strips.
2. Melt butter in a large pan over medium-high heat. Add kale and sauté for about 7 minutes, stirring frequently.
3. Sprinkle with pepper, nutmeg, and flour, stirring until flour has coated kale. Add water, turn heat to low, and cook, covered, for 5 minutes.
4. Remove pan from heat, add carrots, and mix well. Spoon vegetables around chicken in small mounds and serve.

Serves 4

Swiss baked chicken and vegetables (center top, recipe on pages 26 and 27) with stuffing, *Rösti* (right), and onion salad (bottom left, recipe on page 30) will bring raves at family celebrations.

Fried Potatoes
Rösti

Rösti *is so popular in Switzerland that* Röstiteller *are sold everywhere. These ornamental plates, specially designed to serve this round potato cake, are usually so picturesque that they are hung on kitchen walls as decorations. Often they are inscribed with proverbs that differ from canton to canton, just like* Rösti *recipes. In German cantons,* Rösti *is made with onions, elbow macaroni, Appenzeller cheese, or caraway seeds. Italian cantons use rosemary, and the French cantons use tomatoes, sweet paprika, and Gruyère cheese.*

4 large potatoes (2 pounds), boiled in their skins until just tender
2 green onions, chopped
½ teaspoon caraway seeds
½ teaspoon salt
  white pepper to taste
2 tablespoons butter or margarine
2 tablespoons half-and-half

1. When potatoes have cooled, peel and grate coarsely into a large bowl. Add green onions, caraway seeds, salt, and pepper, and mix well.
2. Over medium-high heat, melt butter in a large, non-stick skillet. Add potato mixture and press into a large, compact cake with a spatula. Continue to cook, pressing and compacting the cake, for 3 or 4 minutes.
3. When a nice brown crust forms on the bottom, turn *Rösti* over by sliding it out onto a large plate. Invert the frying pan over the plate. Using pot holders, grip pan and plate together on opposite sides. In one motion, flip the pan and plate so the *Rösti* falls into the pan. (This takes practice, so ask an adult to help at first.)
4. Cook the other side, pressing and compacting the cake, for 3 to 4 minutes.
5. Pour half-and-half evenly over potato cake. Turn heat down to medium low, cover skillet, and cook until the other side turns brown (about 7 minutes).
6. Slide cake onto a plate and serve.

Serves 4

Onion Salad
Zibelsalat

Onions are a celebrated vegetable in the city of Bern, where Zibelmärit *(Onion Market Day) takes place every November. In the 15th century when a rampaging fire almost demolished the city, the first* Zibelmärit *was held for the farmers of nearby Fribourg, who brought onions for the starving inhabitants.*

4 yellow onions (1 pound), peeled and sliced ¼-inch thick
1 teaspoon salt
½ teaspoon pepper
4 bacon slices, chopped
1 tablespoon whole wheat flour
2 tablespoons cider vinegar
dash sugar
2 tablespoons freshly chopped chives

1. In a bowl, sprinkle onion slices with salt and pepper. Using 2 forks, mix well and separate onion slices into separate rings.
2. Place bacon and onion rings in a large skillet over medium heat. Cook until bacon is crisp and onions are light brown (about 10 minutes), stirring frequently.
3. Sprinkle with flour, stirring gently so flour coats onions. Add vinegar and sugar. Cook 2 more minutes, stirring constantly.
4. Remove pan from heat and cover to keep warm. Before serving, sprinkle with chives.

Serves 4

Tomatoes Fribourg Style
Tomates Fribourgeoises

The tomato only found its way into Swiss recipes in the 16th century after Christopher Columbus introduced it to Europe from South America. This recipe, from the canton of Fribourg, uses Gruyère cheese and potatoes as stuffing, whereas, in the canton of Valais seasoned raw eggs are used for stuffing.

2 large tomatoes
2 tablespoons brown sugar

¾ **cup Gruyère or Swiss cheese, finely grated**
2 **cups mashed potatoes (prepared instant or leftovers)**
1 **green onion, chopped**
  dash white pepper
  butter or margarine

1. Preheat oven to 350°.
2. Wash and halve tomatoes. Scoop out most of the flesh (which can be used in the perch recipe) and discard liquid and seeds. Sprinkle each tomato half with ½ tablespoon brown sugar.
3. Mix ½ cup grated cheese with mashed potatoes, white parts of green onion, and pepper. Stuff each tomato with equal amounts. Dot each with a little butter. Place into a well-greased, shallow baking dish and bake for 10 minutes.
4. Remove, sprinkle with remaining cheese, and bake for another 5 minutes.
5. Remove, sprinkle with remaining green onion and serve.

Serves 4

Tomatoes Fribourg style and poached perch fillets (recipe on page 32) combine the flavorful products of Swiss lakes, gardens, and dairies.

Poached Perch Fillets
Filets de Perche

Perch is a delicate freshwater fish found in most lakes in Switzerland. Called Egli *in German-speaking regions and* perche *in French-speaking regions, perch is served with a variety of herb sauces.*

 4 cups water
 **1 whole leek, washed, greens chop-
     ped and white bulb sliced**
 1 teaspoon pickling spice
 ½ teaspoon salt
 **4 pieces perch fillets (about 1 pound),
     fresh or frozen and thawed
     according to package instructions**
 2 tablespoons butter or margarine
 1½ tablespoons white flour
 **⅛ teaspoon dill weed
     dash white pepper**
 2 tablespoons sour cream

1. To make poaching liquid, combine water, leek greens, pickling spice, and salt in a medium-sized pan. Bring to a boil over high heat. Turn heat to medium low and simmer for 30 minutes.

2. Rinse fish fillets under cold water and pat dry with paper towels. Place fillets in a large frying pan, top with cooked leek greens, and pour 1 cup of poaching liquid over fish. Cover and allow to simmer over medium heat for 15 minutes. Scrape leek mixture from fish, remove fillets using a slotted spoon, and place them on a large serving platter. Keep platter of fish in a warm oven until ready to serve.

3. Pour liquid from the pan through a fine sieve and reserve clear stock only.

4. Place butter in a medium-sized pan over medium-high heat. Add white parts of leek and sauté, stirring constantly until leeks are golden.

5. Add flour and stir until flour is light brown. Add 1 cup of reserved fish stock, dill weed, and pepper. Stir to blend well.

6. Remove from heat, add sour cream, and blend. Pour sauce over fish fillets. (Optional: Sprinkle with chopped tomato pieces reserved from tomato recipe.)

Serves 4

Garden-Style Vegetable Salad
Insalata Giardiniera

**1 stalk broccoli, tops and about 2
  inches of stem, washed**
12 cauliflower florets, washed
**1 green onion, white bulb only, finely
  chopped**
**2 tablespoons juice of fresh lemon
  dash salt
  dash white pepper**
1 tablespoon white vinegar
2 tablespoons olive oil
**1 tablespoon finely chopped
  marinated pimento or fresh sweet
  red pepper**
¼ teaspoon dried basil
**4 to 6 lettuce leaves, washed and
  drained**
**4 to 6 pitted black olives, sliced into
  rings**

1. Fill a large cooking pot with 2 inches
of water. Place broccoli and cauliflower
into a steaming basket inside the cooking
pot. Cover and steam over medium-high
heat about 5 to 7 minutes or until vegetables are barely tender.

2. Remove vegetables to a medium-sized
bowl. Add onion, lemon juice, salt, and
pepper.

3. Combine vinegar, oil, pimento, and
basil in a small bowl and stir briskly (or
place in a jar, cover, and shake to mix
well). When vegetables are cool, pour
dressing over them and allow salad to
marinate at room temperature for about
2 hours.

4. When serving, stir and spoon onto 4
small serving plates lined with lettuce
leaves. Garnish with black olive rings.

Serves 4

When served with garden-style vegetable salad (bottom left, recipe on page 33), noodles with saffron make a colorful, authentic Swiss meal.

Noodles with Saffron
Pasta allo Zafferano

½ **pound ground pork**
¼ **teaspoon salt**
¼ **teaspoon white pepper**
½ **teaspoon dried sweet basil**
 3 **cups water**
 1 **chicken bouillon cube**
2½ **tablespoons cornstarch**
¾ **cup heavy cream**
½ **teaspoon saffron strands, loosely packed (or ¼ teaspoon turmeric)**
 9 **ounces fettucini egg noodles**
 2 **tablespoons freshly chopped parsley**
 8 **tablespoons grated Parmesan cheese**

1. In a large skillet, cook pork over medium-high heat, stirring constantly and breaking pork into small pieces.
2. Drain off excess fat and return pork to stove. Lower heat to medium and add salt, pepper, basil, water, and bouillon cube. Simmer for 5 minutes. Bring to a boil.
3. With a fork, stir together cornstarch

and cream in a small bowl. Slowly add this mixture to the boiling pork mixture with a wooden spoon, stirring until mixture becomes thick and creamy (about 1 minute).
4. Turn heat to low and add saffron, stirring until blended. Simmer, uncovered, until ready to serve.
5. Prepare noodles according to package directions. Drain and divide noodles among 4 serving bowls. Ladle saffron sauce over noodles, top with parsley and Parmesan cheese, and serve.

Serves 4

Peek-in-the-Oven Casserole
Ofenguck

**4 large potatoes (about 2 pounds),
    peeled and cut into small cubes
1 small clove garlic
¼ teaspoon salt
½ cup milk
4 tablespoons unsalted butter or
    margarine
¼ teaspoon white pepper
1 cup finely chopped smoked sausage**

**2 green onions, chopped
    pinch dried marjoram
4 eggs
4 tablespoons grated Swiss cheese
2 tablespoons chopped fresh parsley**

1. Cover potato cubes with water in a pan. Add garlic and salt. Bring to a boil over high heat. Lower heat to medium and cook until tender (about 10 minutes).
2. Preheat oven to 375°.
3. Remove potatoes from water and place in a bowl. Discard garlic. Add milk, butter, and white pepper. Mash well. Add sausage, green onions, and marjoram, and mix well.
4. Place potato mixture into a large, well-greased oval casserole dish. With the back of a moist soup spoon, make 4 deep depressions in the potato mixture. Gently break 1 egg into each depression. Bake on oven's middle rack for 20 minutes.
5. Top casserole with grated cheese. Bake for 3 to 5 minutes, or until egg whites are firm. Top with parsley and serve.

Serves 4

Leckerli, cookies from the city of Basel (left, recipe on page 38), are flavored with ginger and other spices. Cherries add color and sweetness to easy-to-make cherry bread pudding (right).

DESSERTS
Nachtisch (G)
Le Déssert (F)
I Dolci (I)

After a brisk hike through the Alps, both tourists and residents love to relax in a Swiss café over coffee and sweets.

Cherry Bread Pudding
Chriesibrägel

Switzerland is rich in cherry orchards. Superb chriesi, *or cherries, harvested each year in June or July, find their way into Swiss candy, cakes, puddings, pies, and preserves.*

3½ **tablespoons unsalted butter or margarine**
 2 **tablespoons** *plus* ¼ **cup white sugar**
 4 **slices white bread, toasted**
1½ **cups hot milk**
 3 **eggs**

⅓ **cup finely ground hazelnuts or walnuts**
 dash nutmeg
1 **tablespoon juice of fresh lemon**
1 **tablespoon grated lemon peel**
1 **16-ounce can dark, sweet, pitted cherries, drained (reserve 4 cherry halves for topping)**
1 **cup heavy cream, whipped (for topping)**

1. Preheat oven to 350°.
2. Grease a medium-sized round casserole dish with ½ tablespoon butter. Sprinkle dish lightly with 2 tablespoons sugar.
3. Cut toasted bread into small cubes and place into a large bowl. Add hot milk and remaining butter and beat until smooth.
4. Add remaining ingredients (except cream), blending well.
5. Pour mixture into prepared baking dish and bake for 40 minutes. Remove from oven and allow to cool slightly.
6. Serve warm. Top each serving with whipped cream and garnish with a cherry half.

Serves 4

Cookies from the City of Basel
Basler Leckerli

Over 600 years ago, trade ships brought spices to the old city of Basel. Among the spices was Ingwer, *or ginger. A bakers' guild, famous for creating new recipes, experimented with the new spice and made what was probably the world's first gingerbread. The street where they worked is named* Imbergässlein, *or "street of spices." Today you can still recognize the street by the spicy aroma that fills the air.*

  1 cup honey
½ cup brown sugar
  1 egg, beaten
¼ teaspoon imitation rum or almond
    extract
2¾ cups whole wheat flour *plus* ¼ cup
    for kneading
1½ tablespoons baking powder
  1 teaspoon ground cinnamon
¼ teaspoon nutmeg
¼ teaspoon ground cloves
¼ teaspoon ground ginger
  1 cup finely ground almonds
  1 tablespoon grated lemon peel

Glaze:
½ cup powdered sugar
  1 tablespoon hot water
⅛ teaspoon imitation rum or almond
    extract

1. Over medium-high heat, bring honey and sugar to a boil in a small saucepan, stirring constantly with a wooden spoon. Remove from heat and transfer to a large glass bowl. Let cool for 20 minutes.
2. Stir egg and extract into honey mixture, mixing well. Slowly add 2¾ cups of flour, the baking powder, cinnamon, nutmeg, cloves, and ginger. Stir in almonds and lemon peel and blend until dough is smooth.
3. Turn dough onto a floured breadboard. Knead, adding in enough remaining flour, until the dough is soft and no longer sticky. Shape into a ball, wrap in plastic wrap, and refrigerate for 2 hours.

4. Preheat oven to 350°.

5. On a lightly floured sheet of aluminum foil, use a rolling pin to roll dough into a 9- by 14-inch rectangle of even thickness. Transfer foil and dough to a 10- by 15-inch baking sheet and place on the middle rack of the oven. Bake about 15 minutes, or until top is golden brown and center springs back when lightly touched. Remove from oven.

6. In a small bowl, mix together all ingredients for glaze. With a pastry brush, spread glaze over the warm *Leckerli*.

7. Lift foil with warm *Leckerli* to a cutting board. Use a sharp knife to cut into 2-inch squares. Remove any remaining foil.

8. Store between sheets of waxed paper in an airtight container for 3 to 4 days before serving.

Makes about 26 cookies

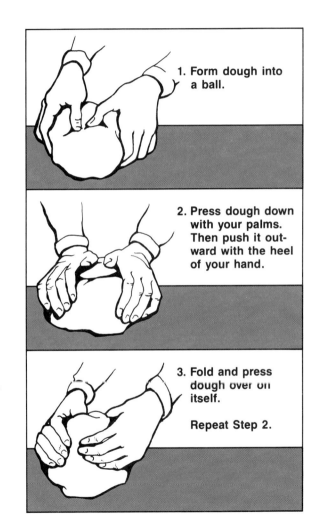

1. Form dough into a ball.

2. Press dough down with your palms. Then push it outward with the heel of your hand.

3. Fold and press dough over on itself.

Repeat Step 2.

Chocolate Fondue
Schokolade Fondue

In 1992, Swiss people ate chocolate at an average rate of 10.6 pounds per person. Swiss chocolate is world famous and many manufacturers guard their formulas in vaults.

12 ounces pound cake, cut into 1-inch cubes
½ cup each of 4 or 5 of the following: pineapples, bananas, pears, or apples, cut into bite-sized chunks whole strawberries or cherries (optional)
½ cup half-and-half
1 tablespoon honey
¼ teaspoon almond extract
6 ounces solid milk chocolate, grated, or milk chocolate morsels
3 ounces solid bittersweet chocolate, grated, or bittersweet chocolate morsels

1. Set fondue pot in the middle of the table with a plate, napkin, a regular fork, and a long fondue fork for each guest. Place cake cubes and fruit (if used) on a serving platter.
2. If using an electric fondue pot, turn setting to "dessert." Add half-and-half, honey, and almond extract, stirring constantly with a wooden spoon until mixture is warm. Add chocolate a little at a time, stirring well until all chocolate has melted. *Note: If using a traditional fondue pot, follow these directions by heating the fondue over a small candle.*
3. Have each person spear cake or fruit with a fondue fork, dip into chocolate, swirl, and remove. Transfer to a regular fork and enjoy.

Serves 4 to 6

At your next party, gather around the table with friends and family for chocolate fondue.

SUPPER
Abendessen (G)
Le Dîner (F)
La Cena (I)

Swiss suppers are generally light meals and are eaten as early as 6 P.M. or as late as 9 P.M. Omelets are favorites in the French regions. The Italian regions enjoy *antipasto* salads of meats, olives, cheeses, or pickled vegetables. Hearty sausages, cold cuts, and cheeses make a supper in the German regions. Throughout the country, evenings are a time for relaxing and entertaining. A popular meal for guests is one of the many varieties of fondue.

Valais-Style Fondue
Fondue Valais

Fondue *comes from the French word*
fondre, *meaning "to melt." The dish was*
probably created around the 15th century
in Swiss peasant homes as a way to use
up hard cheese and stale bread. Now
fondue *is a special treat.*

1 or 2 loaves French bread, cut into
    small cubes, each with some crust
½ pound baked ham, cut into ¾-inch
    cubes (optional)
½ pound Emmentaler cheese, grated
½ pound Gruyère cheese, grated
3 tablespoons white flour
2 cups whole or skim milk
1 tablespoon juice of fresh lemon
    dash sweet paprika

1. Set table in the same manner as for
chocolate fondue. Place bread cubes in a
bread basket lined with a napkin. If used,
place ham cubes on a serving platter.
2. Place both grated cheeses in a large
bowl and sprinkle with flour. Mix lightly
with your hands to coat cheese with flour.
3. If using an electric fondue pot, turn
the setting to "cheese" or "simmer." Pour
in milk and allow to warm. Add lemon
juice and paprika. Then add the cheese
one handful at a time, stirring constantly
and rapidly with a wooden spoon. When
all the cheese is melted, turn heat setting
to "low."
Note: To make fondue without an electric
fondue pot, follow the same directions
using a traditional fondue pot over a
small, denatured alcohol burner. Be sure
to light the burner carefully and adjust
to a small flame. You can also try this
recipe using a double boiler over high
heat. When all cheese has melted, pour
fondue into a serving bowl and place on
a warming tray on the table.
4. Have each person spear a bread cube
through the soft side into the crust, then
dip and swirl the cube in the fondue.
Remove the bread cube, transfer the coated
bread cube to a regular fork, and eat.

Serves 4 to 6

Valais-style fondue with cheese, bread, and ham is a simple supper to serve your family on a weeknight and a treat for guests on a special occasion.

THE CAREFUL COOK

Whenever you cook, there are certain safety rules you must always keep in mind. Even experienced cooks follow these rules when they are in the kitchen.

1. Always wash your hands before handling food.
2. Thoroughly wash all raw vegetables and fruits to remove dirt, chemicals, and insecticides.
3. Use a cutting board when cutting up vegetables and fruits. Don't cut them up in your hand! And be sure to cut in a direction *away* from you and your fingers.
4. Long hair or loose clothing can catch fire if brought near the burners of a stove. If you have long hair, tie it back before you start cooking.
5. Turn all pot handles away from you so that you will not catch your sleeves or jewelry on them. This is especially important when younger brothers and sisters are around. They could easily knock a pot off the stove and get burned.
6. Always use a pot holder to steady hot pots or to take pans out of the oven. Don't use a wet cloth on a hot pan because the steam it produces can burn you.
7. Lift the lid of a steaming pot with the opening away from you so that you will not get burned.
8. If you get burned, hold the burn under cold running water. Do not put grease or butter on it. Cold water helps to take the heat out, but grease or butter will only keep it in.
9. If grease or cooking oil catches fire, throw baking soda or salt at the bottom of the flame to put it out. (Water will *not* put out a grease fire.) Call for help, and try to turn all the stove burners to "off."
10. If you are using a traditional fondue pot with an open flame, ask an adult to help you. Place the candle or burner under the pot before lighting it. Remember to handle matches, candles, and alcohol burners with care.

METRIC CONVERSION CHART

WHEN YOU KNOW		MULTIPLY BY	TO FIND	
MASS (weight)				
ounces	(oz)	28.0	grams	(g)
pounds	(lb)	0.45	kilograms	(kg)
VOLUME				
teaspoons	(tsp)	5.0	milliliters	(ml)
tablespoons	(Tbsp)	15.0	milliliters	
fluid ounces	(oz)	30.0	milliliters	
cup	(c)	0.24	liters	(l)
pint	(pt)	0.47	liters	
quart	(qt)	0.95	liters	
gallon	(gal)	3.8	liters	
TEMPERATURE				
Fahrenheit	(°F)	5/9 (after subtracting 32)	Celsius	(°C)

COMMON MEASURES AND THEIR EQUIVALENTS

3 teaspoons = 1 tablespoon

8 tablespoons = ½ cup

2 cups = 1 pint

2 pints = 1 quart

4 quarts = 1 gallon

16 ounces = 1 pound

INDEX
(recipes indicated by **boldface** type)

ABOUT THE AUTHOR

Helga Hughes received her early culinary training at a private college in Forcheim, Bavaria. After moving to the United States, she wrote cooking articles for national newspapers and magazines, and books on Austrian and vegetarian cooking. When not in the kitchen, Hughes follows her other writing interests—exercise and children—and promotes her books.